Simply Nativity

The traditional Biblical Nativity story
especially written for young children to enjoy

by Jennifer S. Porter
edited by Alison Hedger

"For my dear parents Kit and Walter Howes who gave so much love
and encouragement on our star journey"

Performance time approximately 20 minutes
Suitable for pre-school children, early school years and special education units

TEACHER'S BOOK
Complete with a simple piano part

Illustrations by Hilary Lack

SONGS

1. I Have Some News For You
2. Mary's Song
3. My Father Came From Bethlehem
4. Knock, Knock
5. Mary Wrapped Jesus
6. In The Middle Of The Night
7. One, Two, Three Little Shepherds
8. I Don't Know Where To Go
9. One Wise Man
10. Follow God's Shining Star
11. Hopping Along To Bethlehem

A matching tape cassette of the story and songs is available
and can be used to teach the songs or enjoyed as a listening tape
Order No. GA11041

© Copyright 1997 Golden Apple Productions
A division of Chester Music Limited
8/9 Frith Street, London W1V 5TZ

Order No. GA11040

ISBN 0-7119-6226-X

Rejoice with us as we
celebrate the birth of Jesus.

God sent a message to Mary.
She was to be the mother of Jesus.

1. I HAVE SOME NEWS FOR YOU

Repeat song ad lib

Mary trusted God.
She married a carpenter called Joseph
and together they looked forward
to the baby being born

2. MARY'S SONG

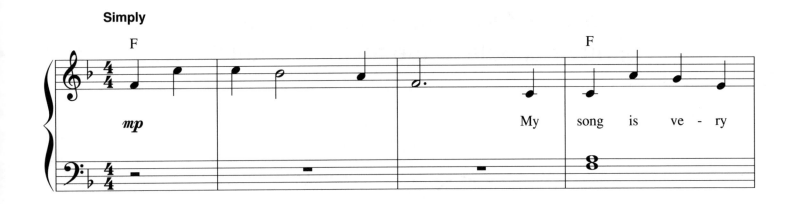

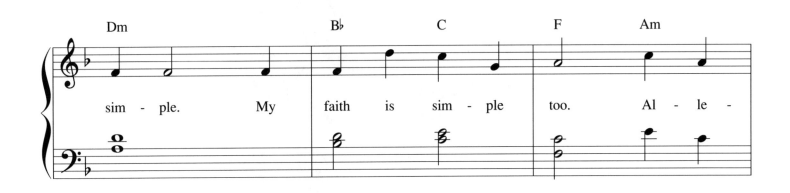

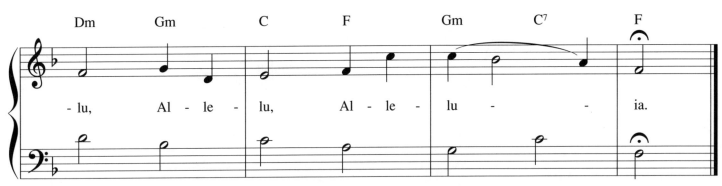

Repeat song ad lib

Not long before the baby was due, all the people were told to go to their father's home town to be counted in a census. Joseph and Mary travelled along with lots of other people to the town of Bethlehem.

3. MY FATHER CAME FROM BETHLEHEM

After the long journey Joseph was anxious for Mary to have a place to stay as her baby was soon to be born. But what a lot of people there were in Bethlehem. The town was crowded. The inns were full.

4. KNOCK, KNOCK

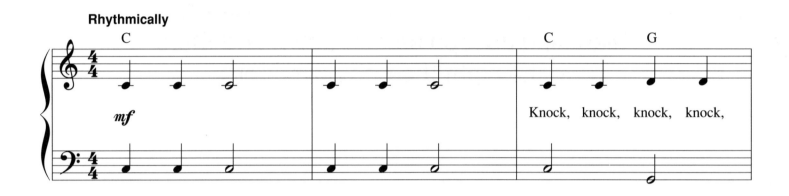

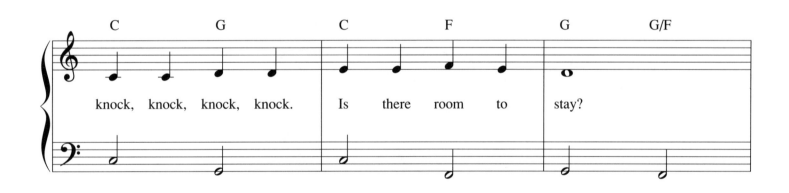

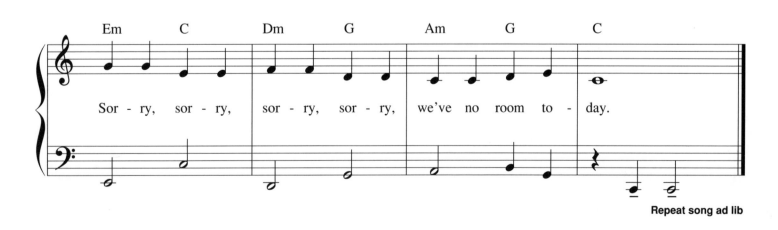

Repeat song ad lib

One innkeeper said
"Would you like to stay in my stable?"
Mary and Joseph answered "Yes please."
In the stable where the animals lived,
Mary and Joseph settled down and there
in the night the baby was born.

5. MARY WRAPPED JESUS

On the hillside outside Bethlehem some shepherds were looking after their sheep. They didn't know the special baby had been born until the angels came and told them.

6. IN THE MIDDLE OF THE NIGHT

When the angels had given their message
the shepherds went into Bethlehem to find
the baby boy.

7. ONE, TWO, THREE LITTLE SHEPHERDS

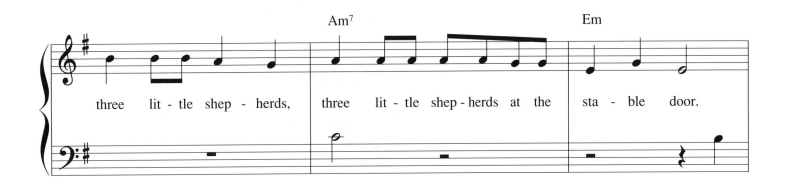

Repeat song ad lib

One little shepherd boy had been fast asleep. He was left behind and didn't know where to go. But the angels helped him.

8. I DON'T KNOW WHERE TO GO

Repeat song ad lib

17

Wise men in the east saw
an amazing new star.
They followed it, knowing that
it must be a sign of something
wonderful.

9. ONE WISE MAN

Everybody can follow the star to find Jesus.

10. FOLLOW GOD'S SHINING STAR

With warmth

Fol - low God's shin - ing star from where - ev - er you are. Some - times high, some - times low. It will lead you to the place where you must go.

Repeat song ad lib

Let's all have fun at Christmas and enjoy ourselves hopping, skipping and jumping for joy!

11. HOPPING ALONG TO BETHLEHEM

For verses 2 and 3 return to introduction

Printed and bound in Great Britain by
Caligraving Limited Thetford Norfolk

7/02 (44766)